The Lotus Europa was produced between 1ξ
Colin Chapman, the design objectives were 1
outstanding good looks with the now famous Lotus standards of road holding,
safety, and reliability." Originally planned to replace the Lotus Seven, and slotting
into the existing range below the Elan as a low-cost sports/GT car, it mirrored the
then-current competition trend for a mid-mounted engine. The Europa was an
outstanding car in its own right, offering the customer a very different vehicle to
the Elan.

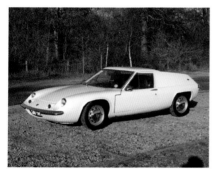

The Europa Series 2 was Lotus' first revision of its 1960s mid-engined masterpiece. Similar in appearance to the Series 1, it had a number of mechanical and cosmetic tweaks.

Using the template pioneered with the Lotus Elan, which became the standard configuration for Lotus road cars of the '60s, '70s, and '80s, the Europa had a glass fibre bodyshell placed on a lightweight steel backbone chassis.

Initially, the Europa was offered to the continental market in left-hand drive, fitted with a 1470cc 78bhp four-cylinder engine, and transaxle from the Renault 16. Always a strict two-seater, the early Europa's defining feature was the tall flat rear deck with a pair of high buttresses each side, which reduced the rear three-quarter view from the letterbox sized rear window to next to nothing. At first, the bodyshell was bonded to the chassis and featured an innovative ventilation system, requiring the side windows to be fixed, and proved to be very inconvenient in typical day-to-day use.

A racing version, the Lotus 47, was introduced alongside the Series 1 in 1967. Powered by the famous Lotus Twin Cam engine linked to a Hewland transaxle, it was aimed at GT Group 4 racing. The Lotus 47 is a specialist vehicle and is outside the scope of this book.

The Europa's backbone chassis is made from folded steel sheet. At the front, a fabricated crossmember carries the suspension, while a V-shaped cradle at the rear holds the engine and gearbox.

The Series 2 Europa, introduced in July 1968, had many improvements over the Series 1, not least bolting the body to the chassis and electrically operated door windows. Still powered by Renault, the Series 2 was made available to the UK market as a right-hand drive. Priced about 15 per cent cheaper than a factory Lotus Elan Series 4, but around 15 per cent more expensive than an Elan in kit form. The Series 2 Europa, marketed as an alternative rather than a rival to the front-engined Elan, was a welcome addition to the UK market as the only mid-engined sports car produced in Britain.

The Twin Cam replaced the Series 2 and was powered by the famous Lotus Twin Cam engine. The rear buttresses were cut down to improve visibility.

Lotus embarked on a major revision to the Europa in 1971. The Renault engine was replaced with a 105bhp Lotus Twin Cam unit while retaining the Renault transaxle, the three-quarter rear view was improved by cutting down the buttresses, and the bodyshell was modified to enhance the passenger accommodation. The result was the Europa Twin Cam.

The fitting of a 126bhp Lotus big-valve Twin Cam engine resulted in the last-of-the-line Europa Twin Cam Special, and at the same time, a new 5-speed transaxle from Renault was offered as an option. The Europa is a delicate and potentially fragile car, built with Chapman's adage of 'add lightness' firmly in mind. While a good Europa is a delight to drive and own, finding one is not so easy. Even though the cars are probably past the 'banger' stage, when buying one, you must be careful. You need to understand that the Europa is not just another sports car, but a finely crafted, carefully engineered classic, and does not respond well to ham-fisted or careless owners/mechanics. This book will help prospective owners understand the subtleties of Europa ownership, and will help to guide them towards finding a great example.

The final iteration was the Twin Cam Special. Fitted with the big-valve version of the Twin Cam, it also had the option of a five-speed gearbox.

Acknowledgements
The author would like to thank the following Europa owners who allowed their cars to be viewed and photographed: Rob Aylott, Steve Carpenter, Mike Hamlin, Andrew Komosa, Geoff Morgan, Gary Morris, John Rand, and Martin Ricketts. Thanks are also due to the folks at Club Lotus, and my wife and daughter for putting up with me while writing another book.

Contents

The Essential Buyer's Guide™ currency
At the time of publication a BG unit of currency "⬤" equals approximately
£1.00/US$1.33/Euro 1.13. Please adjust to suit current exchange rates.

1 Is it the right car for you?
– marriage guidance

Do you fit in the car?
First and foremost, you must check out an example to see if you fit in it. The cabins of the early Series 1 and 2 are snug, to say the least, and the hammock-style seats mean you sit in a reclined 'racing car' position. In Series 1 cars, the seats are fixed, and you have to physically unbolt and move the pedals to achieve a comfortable seating position. The seats in the Series 2 move forwards and backwards, but there is not much travel. The later Twin Cam has a slightly longer and deeper cockpit, which does give more room, but the seats are still hammock-style. The second aspect is the height of the seats. At a mere 42.5in (108cm), the car is very low, and the seats are low, too. This makes getting in and out of the vehicle interesting, and usually quite undignified for those less flexible!

The Europa is low, and larger drivers may find it a bit of a squeeze to get in and out. But once seated, the cockpit is excellent.

Driving
The Europa has the benefit of Colin Chapman's design genius, but it's still a 1960s sports car. While the suspension gives long travel, soft springing, and well-controlled damping, the ride is not limousine-smooth. The steering is sharp and direct, and the engine is positioned just behind the occupants' heads, so can be heard and felt. On the road, the Europa should be a joy to drive, giving an involving and engaging experience that is miles away from a anodyne modern hatchback. These elements mark out the nature of the car: it is designed to be driven fast and well – factors that add to the overall owner experience.

With its mid-mounted engine and race-bred suspension, the Europa's handling and ride are excellent, and streets ahead of most rivals.

Luggage capacity

Designed as a GT car, the Europa is not a large vehicle, and to be honest, you are probably better off sending your luggage ahead if you are planning to undertake a long tour. The small front luggage compartment is irregularly shaped and can take a couple of small squashy overnight bags. The rear luggage compartment offers a mere 2ft³ (0.056m³) of space, is sited over the transmission, and gets hot. Inside the cabin there is a small glovebox, but there is no space for luggage, other than the passenger seat if a passenger isn't present.

Home maintenance

Despite being an exotic mid-engined GT sports car, the Europa is relatively easy to maintain at home. Thanks to Lotus' 'parts bin' approach to sourcing components, there are not too many bespoke parts that require regular attention. With the Renault-engine cars, routine maintenance is not too difficult; all the belt drives are on the rear of the engine, while the carburettor and distributor are easy to access. The Twin Cam offers some challenges, especially with the drivebelt to the water pump, and the water pump itself, which is buried in the timing cover tightly against the bulkhead. Also, the distributor and oil filter are buried under the carburettors. The front suspension derives from the Triumph Herald, and while the lower trunnions need regular oiling or greasing, the rest is pretty

The Europa's front luggage locker is small, and filling it with luggage can interfere with airflow to the cabin.

The Twin Cam engine is relatively easy to work on, and apart from accessing the front-mounted water pump, the installation has plenty of room for maintenance.

reliable and easily accessible. The rear suspension is all Lotus and relatively simple to maintain, the driveshaft universal joints need regular greasing, but the rest only requires routine inspection; replacing bushes and wheel bearings when they wear.

Will it fit in your garage?
The good news is that the Europa's overall length of 13ft 1.5in (400.05cm), width of 5ft 4.5in (164cm), and height of 42.5in (108cm), means it will fit in all but the smallest garages.

Plus points
The Europa is a massively accomplished small GT car, which can be incredibly rewarding to own. Its roadholding and handling is up to Lotus' usual high standard, and its small size makes it wieldy and manoeuvrable. The car has bags of style and is rare, while the glass fibre body is rust free.

Minus points
The car has a small cabin and is very low, making getting in and out in a dignified manner difficult! Due to its age and glass fibre bodyshell, it can suffer from obscure and difficult to diagnose electrical problems. As a 1960s design, the car needs regular servicing and sympathetic handling if it's to give its best. The chassis can rust, and the body and paint are not immune to deterioration. The Lotus Twin Cam engine can also be a bit of an oil leaker.

Alternatives
There are only a few mid-engined alternatives to the Europa from the '60s and '70s: the Lotus Esprit, which replaced the Europa; Porsche 914/916, Matra-Simca Bagheera, and the exceedingly rare De Tomaso Valleluna. If you widen the criteria to two-seater sports coupés with a decent pedigree, the Lotus Elan, and the slightly larger Plus 2, are probably the best alternatives. But don't discount the MGB GT or Triumph GT6.

If you don't want a mid-engined car, the Lotus Elan is a viable alternative. It has the benefit of being a soft top, and, just like the Europa, it has the Lotus Twin Cam engine, race-bred suspension, and a corrosion-free glass fibre body.

The Lotus Esprit replaced the Europa. Retaining the glass fibre body and steel backbone chassis of the Europa, the Esprit has classic 1970s wedge styling and the Lotus 900-series engine.

2 Cost considerations

– affordable, or a money pit?

Servicing

Lotus recommends that service intervals are frequent, reflecting the Europa's delicate nature and 1960s ancestry. However, regular servicing of the Europa is straightforward, especially the Renault-engined Series 1 and 2, and well within the ability of a competent home mechanic. While servicing the Ford-based Twin Cam engine is also straightforward, changing the timing chain (there is no set period, but expect it to need replacing every 50,000-75,000 miles) and setting the tappets are head-off jobs. If you are contemplating these tasks, then its worth taking the engine out to change the water pump at the same time.

The Renault-engined cars need an 'A' service every 3000 miles/5000km or two months, a more rigorous 'B' service every 5000 miles/10,000km or six months, and a comprehensive 'C' service every 12,000 miles/20,000km or 12 months.

Recommended service intervals for Twin Cam variants are every 5000 miles/8000km or three months when an 'A' type service is required, and a more rigorous 'B' type service is due every 10000 miles/16,000km or six months. Emissions equipped Twin Cam engines require additional services to the carburettor every 12,000 miles/20,000km and every 24,000 miles/40,000km.

Mechanical

Engine

Oil filter: ●x7
Thermostat: ●x6
Water pump repair kit
    (Twin Cam/Special): ●x35
Water pump (Renault): ●x75
Timing chain (Twin Cam/Special): ●x19.50
Timing chain tensioner: ●x35
Piston set (Twin Cam/Special): ●x480
Piston ring set (Twin Cam/Special): ●x120
Big end bearing set
    (Twin Cam/Special): ●x41
Main bearing set (Twin Cam/Special): ●x67
Camshaft bearing set
    (Twin Cam/Special): ●x100
Valve guides (Twin Cam/Special): ●x8
Valves (Twin Cam/Special): ●x11
Gasket set (Twin Cam/Special): ●x41
Dellorto carb refurbishment kit: ●x55
Twin Cam rebuild: ●x5000

Clutch

Clutch cable (Series 1 and 2 RHD): ●x37
Clutch cable (Twin Cam/Special): ●x62
Clutch plate: ●x120
Clutch cover: ●x160
Clutch release bearing
    (Twin Cam/Special): ●x20

Brakes

Master cylinder repair kit: ●x10.5
Master cylinder: ●x74
Master cylinder (Dual Circuit): ●x170

The Europa's engine bay affords pretty good access to the engine and gearbox. The Renault engine has its ancillary drives positioned at the rear, making maintenance easy.

Front brake pads: ●x13
Front brake calliper rebuild Kit: ●x13
Front brake calliper piston: ●x12.50
Front brake calliper exchange: ●x50
Front brake disc ●x12.50
Rear brake shoes
    (Series 1/Twin Cam): ●x30
Rear brake shoes (Special): ●x32.50
Rear brake cylinder
    (Series 1/Twin Cam): ●x10.50
Rear brake cylinder (Special): ●x20
Rear brake drum (Special): ●x40

Suspension
Front trunnions: ●x17.50
Front vertical link: ●x87.50
Top ball joint: ●x9.50
Track rod end: ●x12.50
Front shock absorber
    (Series 1/ 2): ●x100
Front shock absorber
    (Series 2/Twin Cam/Special): ●x115
Rear shock absorber: ●x95

Miscellaneous
Alternator (Twin Cam/Special): ●x60
Alternator belt (Twin Cam/Special): ●x5
Radiator (alloy): ●x140

Body parts
Europa body panels and complete
bodyshells are available. They are
mostly made to order, which is when
prices tend to be quoted.

The Twin Cam engine is tight against the
bulkhead, limiting access to the water
pump and cam chain. This example is
fitted to the Twin Cam Special, and is
one of the last with a big-valve head.

Chassis: ●x2495
Headlight: ●x12
Front indicator
    (Series 2/Twin Cam/Special): ●x20
Rear light (Twin Cam/Special): ●x195
Rear light lens (Twin Cam/Special): ●x37
Door handle (Twin Cam/Special): ●x42

Hard to find parts
All Europa variants are pretty well served
for parts. The main area of concern is
the transmission, where it seems that
parts availability is poor. Virtually every
part of the Twin Cam engine is readily
available. Parts to rebuild Renault units
are harder to find, but specialists are
starting to have some components
re-manufactured. Original cabin trim
is also getting hard to find, but as
the interior is relatively simple to put
together, any competent trimmer should
be able to duplicate the original design.
Series 1 rear lights, as used by Lancia,
are hard to find.

A Renault gearbox or transaxle is fitted
to all Europas. This is a Series 2 unit and
shows the good access available
once the luggage box is lifted out.

3 Living with a Europa
– will you get along together?

From the rear, the Europa is unmistakable. The unique styling helps to give it a dedicated and enthusiastic following.

The Europa is a mid-engined Grand Touring sports car, designed to transport two people over a long distance in relative comfort and speed. Back in the '60s and '70s, factory testing often involved weekend trips to northern Italy, which the Europa achieved easily. One early road test consisted of driving the car from the UK to Sicily and back, with few problems.

The Europa is all about its handling. The mid-engined configuration gives it great balance, imparting it with handling and roadholding that would not disgrace a modern day sports car. However, even with Chapman's genius behind it, the design is still governed by the laws of physics, and, the relatively skinny tyres do limit its grip.

Once you're in the Europa, the cabin is nicely fitted out, and the driving position is excellent. This is a Series 2, with its wooden dash and wide centre console.

11

This Twin Cam has been resprayed in the classic Lotus 'Gold Leaf' racing colours of red over white, giving it a striking appearance.

All Europa engines are great units with a certain amount of character (read 'noise') inherent in its design and positioning, which adds to the driving experience. Whether it's powered by the Lotus Twin Cam or Renault unit, the car's performance is good for its age and engine size, and it will hold its own in modern traffic. The ride is surprisingly compliant as roadholding and handling is achieved through carefully controlled-damping, long travel, and relatively soft springing. As the brakes have such little weight to haul down from speed, they work well, despite the basic specification.

Any Europa cockpit is a nice place to be: reclined 'race car' seating position, cosy but cosseting layout, and workmanlike fixtures and fittings. Internally, the Series 1 cockpit is sparsely furnished, the alloy dashboard and fixed seats are in line with its cheap and cheerful ethos, but it still has a full set of instruments. The Series 2 is a bit better appointed: not luxurious but nicely finished in a skilled fashion with better seats, carpets, and a wooden dash, most of which was carried over to the Twin Cam and Special. The heating and ventilation system could be better, but it does work, and judicious use of the standard electric windows on the Series 2 and onwards helps enormously. While there is little spare room in the cabin when there is a driver and passenger, the front and rear compartments can accommodate a reasonable amount of luggage. Mind you, the rear compartment does get hot from the engine, and if you fill the front section, it can block the air intakes that supply the cabin.

In the last-of-the-line Twin Cam Special, the interior has a little more room than the Series 2, and is even more luxuriously appointed.

Spares are generally available. Supply is good for the Twin Cam engine, but not so good for the Renault unit; the availability of parts for the transmission can present some challenges. Body panels are obtainable; so are a complete bodyshell and chassis. Service items and suspension bushes are all readily available, along with wheel bearings and suspension swivels. There are plenty of good Lotus clubs and web resources dedicated to the Europa, making it much easier for new owners to get answers to questions, and to build their knowledge of the car.

Today the Europa is a rare classic that attracts attention wherever it goes. It'll give the owner superlative handling, roadholding, and good performance, but it's also small, cramped, and hard to get in and out of.

4 Relative values

– which model for you?

In the Europa world, condition is everything, and it dictates the price of any car. On a theoretical level, there are four basic models: Renault-powered Series 1 and 2, Lotus-engined Twin Cam, and Twin Cam Special. However, the cut-off between the Series 1 and 2 cars is not clean, and it is not uncommon to find a Series 2 vehicle that shares elements of a Series 1. In general, the market value of a Series 2 will tend to be about 10 per cent lower than that of an equivalent Series 1 and Twin Cam, while the Twin Cam Special, with the big-valve engine, will be 5 to 10 per cent more than an equivalent Twin Cam. The ultimate Europa is a Twin Cam Special with the optional five-speed gearbox. It'll cost 5 to 15 per cent more than an equivalent four-speed car. A very early and original Series 1 will command a value around 10 per cent higher than a later Series 1, Twin Cam, or four-speed Special.

The Series 1 (Lotus designation Type 46) was introduced in December 1968 and produced almost exclusively as a left-hand drive car. Powered by a Renault 1470cc four-cylinder engine and fitted with the Renault Type 336 gearbox, its bodyshell was bonded to the chassis, had high rear buttresses, fixed seats and adjustable foot

The Series 1 from 1966 to 1968 had the chassis bonded to the body, and was produced in left-hand drive format only.

The rear lights on the Series 1 were sourced from Lancia, and are now hard to find. Note, the high rear buttresses restrict rear three-quarter visibility.

pedals, as well as exterior door push buttons recessed in the body, enabling the rear edge of the door to be used to open it. Early cars had one-piece perspex fixed door windows, while later cars had clip-in removable side windows; the factory marketed a kit to retrofit them. The rear light clusters were sourced from Lancia, and the majority of early cars had front indicators mounted on the outside edge of the wings. The Series 1A, or Mk2, was introduced in the latter half of 1967, had removable windows as standard, fixed quarter lights, and the option of having a factory-fitted brake servo. In early 1966 the Series 1B was introduced, sources say it had Lucas rear lights and possibly a wood dashboard. Some cars, including the prototypes, were fitted with

From the rear, the Series 2's prominent rear buttresses are evident, as well as the Lucas rear lights shared with the Elan and Plus 2.

additional rectangular side and indicator lights sourced from the Renault 10 and 16, which were positioned under each end of the front bumper.

Introduced in August 1968, the Series 2 (Lotus designation Type 54) replaced the Series 1, and from July 1969, was offered to the UK market in right-hand drive form. The main changes were the bodyshell, which was now bolted to the chassis, making accident damage easier and cheaper to repair; a revised floor moulding, to allow for adjustable seats; and electric side windows, getting rid of the clumsy pop out units. The doors also had triangular fixed front-quarter lights, which on early cars were made from perspex. Later cars were fitted with a new door lock mechanism. Chrome handles replaced the recessed push buttons at the rear of the door, although some of the early Series 2 cars still had the Series 1 door locks. The new rear light units were large

Twin Cam Special was powered by the big-valve Twin Cam engine, and had many detailed improvements, including a lowered floor to give more cabin room.

Lucas parts and were shared with the Elan/Plus 2 (as well as the earlier S1B). On later examples, the under-bumper front indicators were replaced with round units located in recesses just above the bumper. Note that the transition from the Series 1 to Series 2 was not a clear cut-off, with some Series 2 cars having Series 1 features as described above.

The Series 2 Federal (Lotus designation Type 65), introduced in March 1969, was produced for the US market. The car had minor specification changes from the Series 2: a larger 1565cc Renault engine; twin windscreen wipers; a modified chassis; front wishbones; alternative front springs and dampers to raise the headlamp height, along with different rated rear dampers and springs; a steering lock; and a buzzer to warn that the ignition is on.

Introduced in October 1971, the Twin Cam (Lotus designation Type 74) superseded the Series 2 and Series 2 Federal, and was powered by the Lotus Twin Cam engine in a standard 105bhp specification. The main

The front end of the Twin Cam Special is shared with the Series 2; the indicators above the bumper are distinctive.

distinguishing points from the Series 2 was the cutting down of the rear buttresses to improve rear three-quarter visibility, and an extra inch added to the wheelbase. The floor of the passenger compartment was lowered, and the seats changed, giving a bit more room. While the gear change mechanism was improved and the chassis strengthened, the suspension mounting points were revised so the front end could be raised to meet US headlamp height legislation. The engine cover on the Twin Cam had only two air intake grilles, one on each side, distinguishing it from the Renault-engined variant. The cars were also fitted with a small chin spoiler to cut front end lift. A Renault Type 352 four-speed gearbox with a revised change mechanism was introduced at the early stage of Twin Cam production.

The Twin Cam Special (sharing the Lotus Type 74 designation with the Twin Cam), introduced in August 1972, was fitted with the Lotus big-valve Twin Cam engine, and had the option of the new Renault Type 365 five-speed gearbox based on the unit in the Renault 12 Gordini and Renault 16 TS. The Twin Cam Special was the final production version of the Europa and was a fitting swan song, its 126bhp engine gave the car a sparkling performance, and the five-speed box aided motorway use. The Europa ceased production in September 1975.

In appearance, The Twin Cam and Twin Cam Special are identical, apart from the badges. Yellow is Lotus' traditional colour.

Once you've found what appears to be a good car, it's well worth the effort to ask the vendor some searching questions before viewing, ensuring it's what you want to buy and to avoid a wasted journey. The location of the car is significant. A local vehicle may be worth a look if only to build your knowledge of the Europa, giving you a benchmark against which you can compare other cars, although it may, of course, be exactly what you want. If it's a long way away, the cost of getting there, in terms of travel and time, may be significant.

Dealer or private sale?

Establish if an owner or dealer is selling the car. If the owner is selling it privately, you have little legal recourse if you buy it and subsequently find problems. In the UK, it's very much the case of 'caveat emptor,' or 'buyer beware'. Buying from a dealer, you should benefit from a significant level of legal protection, and usually a warranty or guarantee of sorts. Owners should be able to provide you with details of the car's history in both written and verbal form. Dealers will probably hold some information, but will not have as much knowledge about the vehicle's history.

Cost of collection and delivery?

It's worth working out the cost of collection and delivery of the car, especially if it's a long way away. Even if you are proposing to drive the car home, you still need to get to the vendor, which could require a lift or use of public transport. The cost of having the car transported to your base may be cheaper than you expect if you use a web-based courier/car collection portal: These can be found by searching the web for 'car shipping.' In the UK, and worldwide, many companies specialise in

Indicators on the Series 2 and onwards are positioned in the front panel.

moving cars on low loaders, and offer surprisingly low rates.

Viewing: when and where?

When viewing any car, it's important to go to the seller's address or business premises. If they suggest meeting in a public area, like a carpark or motorway services, regard this with caution. If the car is viewed privately at a seller's home, make sure the vehicle's documentation is in the seller's name and displays the address where you are viewing the car.

This Europa Twin Cam Special was pictured at a Castle Coombe Club Lotus track day.

For a business sale, the vendor should have the registration documentation. View the car in daylight, and give yourself plenty of time to carry out the checks outlined below. If it's raining, be very careful, as a wet car can conceal poor paintwork.

Reason for sale?
Ask the seller why they are selling and how long they have been the owner. There are many legitimate reasons, and it is always worth seeing if the answer is plausible.

Left-hand to right-hand drive
Ask if the car has been converted to right-hand drive (or vice versa), and, if so, was the conversion done professionally. While the Europa is relatively easy to convert, it does compromise originality. However, if you are in the UK or Australia, and really want a Series 1, then left-hand drive or a conversion are the only options.

Condition – (body/chassis/mechanical/interior)
Ask the seller to describe of the overall condition of the car, and ask if there are any problems. While the seller's opinion of what good condition is may differ from yours, most are honest and will give you an idea of what to expect.

All original specification?
Verify if the car is original. Is it still in its original factory colour? Does it have the original engine, chassis, interior, and bodyshell? What modifications have been applied? Does the owner have a Lotus Heritage certificate to confirm the original factory specifications, along with the unit, engine, and transmission numbers?

Chassis and engine numbers?
Do the chassis and engine numbers, as well as the Vehicle Identification Number (VIN), match the registration document, and, if available, the Lotus Heritage certificate? If not, ask why.

Matching data/legal
For a private sale, ask if the seller owns the car and if their name and address is on the registration document. If not, ask why and verify the answer. For example, if a vendor is selling the car on behalf of the owner, ask to be put in touch or meet with them. If the owner is selling the car, then ask to see identification to verify their identity.

The Special's rear lights were shared with the Elan and Plus 2, and the rear bumper is from a Ford Cortina Mk2.

For those countries that require an annual test of roadworthiness, does the car have a document showing it complies (an MoT certificate in the UK, which can be verified on 0300 123 9000)?

In the UK, there are a number of companies that carry out checks on vehicles based on its registration number. They can identify if a vehicle is stolen, an insurance write-off, or if any outstanding finance is owed. In the UK, these organisations can supply vehicle data:

DVSA 0300 123 9000   HPI 0845 300 8905   AA 0344 209 0754
DVLA 0844 306 9203   RAC 0330 159 0364

There are many customised Europas. This example has non-standard lights and bodywork modifications to give it a different, but still classic, look.

From the rear, the Europa's lines are apparent. This Twin Cam Special shows the cut-down rear buttresses.

Unleaded fuel

Built with cast iron valve seats cast into its alloy head. The consensus is that it will run happily on unleaded fuel, but high revs can cause valve seat recession. For total peace of mind, there are additives available, or companies who will replace the existing valve seats with new ones.

Insurance

In the UK, before you can drive the car on the road, you must have insurance in place. Many insurance companies can pre-arrange cover, activating it over the phone if you decide to buy it. If you take the car out for a test drive make, sure you are covered.

How can you pay?

Ask the vendor how they want you to pay. Cash is king, and waving a wad of notes will often get the buyer a discount. Bank transfers, cheques, and bank drafts are all safer than carrying a large amount of cash. Most sellers will want to make sure that funds have cleared before releasing the car.

Professional vehicle check (mechanical examination)

If you do not feel that you have the skills or confidence to carry out a mechanical inspection, there are organisations and individuals that can, for a fee. There are motoring organisations in most countries that will carry out vehicle checks, but in the case of a specialist classic car, you are better off going to a marque specialist or engaging a knowledgeable friend to inspect the vehicle. Organisations that will carry out a general professional check in the UK are:

AA 0800 056 8040 (motoring organisation with vehicle inspectors)
RAC 0330 159 0720 (motoring organisation with vehicle inspectors)

6 Inspection equipment
– these items will really help

This book
Reading glasses
Notebook and pencil
Overalls
Trolley jack, blocks of wood, chocks and axle stands
Fridge Magnet
Strong magnet on a telescopic stick
Torch or headtorch and a handheld LED light
Digital camera or camera phone
Mirror on a stick
Probe – a small screwdriver is ideal
Small pry bar or large screwdriver
Stethoscope or long screwdriver
Engine compression tester and plug spanner
A friend or marque specialist

This book is designed to give you a structured approach to assessing a car, so make sure you have read it and understand how to use it. The quick checks in chapter 8 along with the in-depth checks and checkboxes in chapter 9 will guide you through the assessment process, making sure you don't miss anything.

If you need reading glasses for close work, then make sure you have them with you. The notebook and pencil are used to jot down information as you inspect the car. For example, if you use the compression tester, you can write down the

readings. Your overalls will show you mean business and will protect your clothes while you are rolling around on the ground inspecting the oily bits!

Hopefully, the owner will have a jack, but bringing your own trolley jack and axle stands means there is no excuse for not getting the car up in the air for an inspection. Use the wood blocks to prevent damage to the vehicle when jacking it up, using the front chassis crossmember or the factory jacking points, and making sure you don't cause any damage. Chock the wheels to stop the car rolling off the jack, using axle stands to ensure the car is still supported if the jack fails.

While a fridge magnet won't help to assess the integrity of the Europa's glass fibre bodyshell, both the fridge and telescopic stick magnet should be used on the various points where the chassis is exposed, making sure it's all metal.

The torch should be one that can give you a focussed beam of light to allow you to peer into any tight spots, such as the gaps between the bodyshell and the chassis. The handheld LED lamp or headtorch should give a spread beam of light that will make peering under the car and in wheelarches easier, enabling you to pick up any problems. The digital camera or phone camera can be used to take pictures of inaccessible areas, which you can then view on the screen. They can be used to take pictures of areas you are not sure about and may need to examine further. It's also useful to take photos of the VIN plate and registration document so you can research the car at your leisure. The mirror is useful to take a look at areas that are relatively inaccessible.

Use the probe to poke at anything that looks suspicious, such as parts of the chassis that look corroded, or corrosion on the rear radius arms. The pry bar is used to check for excessive play in suspension bushes and swivels.

Stethoscopes are useful to locate where any strange noises in the engine are originating. You can also use a long screwdriver as a stethoscope by placing the handle against your ear and the head of the driver on the engine where you think the noise is coming from, but beware moving parts.

The compression tester is used to assess the engine's overall condition and identify problems with individual cylinders.

Finally, take along a friend or marque specialist who can give you a second opinion on any immediate queries. They'll be able to provide an objective and unemotional view, helping you to decide if the car is the one for you.

7 Fifteen minute evaluation
– walk away or stay?

Introduction
The initial inspection should take around fifteen minutes. It will tell you if the car is what it says it is, if it's in a condition that warrants detailed scrutiny, and if it may be the vehicle for you. Try to view the car with a cold engine, so when it's started up, you can hear any knocks or rattles, and see if it does start easily. Also, it's a lot easier to assess a cold engine and cooling system, as you won't burn your hands on hot components.

The VIN plate on a Europa should be on the rear face of the front luggage compartment bulkhead.

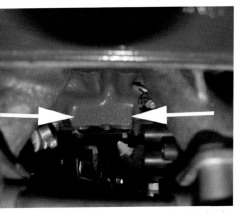

The Twin Cam engine number is sited underneath the carburettor, on a flat lug just above the engine mount.

The owner and numbers check
Check both the VIN and engine number in the car's documentation (V5C in the UK), which should match the numbers on the car's VIN plate and the engine. If they don't, and the vendor can't provide a very good reason why, don't buy the car. If you are buying from a private seller, their name and address should be on the registration document, and you should check that these are accurate. Ask to see their driving licence and view the car at the address in the registration document. Again, if they don't match, or something doesn't add up, walk away.

The car's VIN, engine, and transmission numbers are on the dataplate, which is usually mounted on the back panel of the front luggage locker. Renault engine numbers are found on the cylinder block, under the exhaust manifold, and above the starter. The transmission number is on the top rear of the case by the rear mount. The engine number on the Twin Cam is stamped just above the engine mount, on the carburettor side. There may be a chassis number stamped on the right rear upper face of the frame, beside the engine. In the engine bay, a body number could be moulded into the front edge of the top of the body. Note, these are internal Lotus numbers, and will not match the VIN on the dataplate.

There are a number of companies that will carry out a data check for a small fee. While this is typically used to find out

This Twin Cam shows the correct ride height and stance.

if a newer car has outstanding finance, it will also reveal if it's been stolen or written-off, so it's worth having one done. In the UK, the DVLA offers various checks based on a vehicle's registration number, and again, this free online service can be useful to check if the car is what it is supposed to be. If you run the registration number, the make and colour can be confirmed. The current MoT status can also be seen, and the site will allow you to look at its MoT history from 2005.

Finally, a Lotus Heritage certificate should show the original numbers, paint, colour, and ex-factory date.

The walk-around

Take your time when walking around the car and look for any problems. At this stage, it is useful to identify any damage or faults with the exterior of the vehicle.

What does the paint look like, is it dull or nicely polished? Are there any major blistering or micro blisters? Is it all the same shade? If there are pinstripes, are they all there? If the car has recently been resprayed, asked for evidence that it has been done correctly.

Does the car sit square to the ground, or is one side or corner lower than the other? Are the wheels square in the arches, with equal gaps between the tyres and bodyshell, and are the gaps the same each side? Do the wheels have the same camber on each side? If not, further investigation is needed.

Do the doors, bonnet, and boot lid fit with even panel gaps? Do they open cleanly without drooping? Do the locks and catches work smoothly, and do they close easily? Are there any gaps where the doors meet the seals? Are the chrome window surrounds still in good condition? Is all the brightwork present? Check if the bumpers are dent- and rust-free, is the chrome is in good condition? Check if the windscreen

is free of cracks and scratches, and if the windscreen wiper(s) are present and in good condition. Is there a sunroof, and, if so, does it look original or aftermarket; moonroofs were popular fitments in the '80s and '90s, is it in good condition? Are the rear lights correct for the car; small Lancia units were fitted to the Series 1, larger oblong Lucas units on the Series 2 and Twin Cam. Check that the lenses are crack free and not crazed.

The Series 1 has an austere interior, alloy-faced dash, and minimal trim. All production Series 1 cars were left-hand drive.

The interior

There's not much to the Europa's interior: just enough room for a couple of passengers, the controls, and instruments! Inside the car, does it smell musty or damp? Check the condition of the carpets and see if they are worn or wet. Are the seats in a good state? Are the covers split? Are all the instruments present, in good order, and working? Is the headlining in good shape? Finally, check the door trim and operation of the door locks and windows.

While the interior is small, it can still become tatty. This immaculate example of a Special shows how the interior of a Series 2 and Twin Cam *should* look.

Under the bonnet

There are a couple of important things to look for under the front bonnet. The radiator lives in the front right-hand corner of the front compartment. You should check it for any signs of leakage, and whether it is cold. Check the coolant level and its condition. Antifreeze is a must in both Renault and Lotus engines, and the coolant should not show any signs of oil contamination. Rusty coolant implies a lack of regular changes. The front compartment should hold the spare wheel, while the car's VIN plate should be mounted on the rear of the middle bulkhead. There may be evidence of accident damage to the bodyshell. While this is not a problem if it has been repaired correctly, any repairs should be neat, unobtrusive, and with minimal filler.

The engine bay

Under the boot lid, the engine bay should be clean and tidy, with no evidence of obvious mistreatment. Use the pictures in this book to make sure everything that should be there is present. For example, airboxes and filters are often discarded in the search for more performance. If the car is a Twin Cam, does it have the correct carburettor? Until late 1971, most UK Twin Cam variants came with a Stromberg unit, and then a Dellorto. All US Federal emissions vehicles came equipped with a Stromberg unit. In late 1971, some of the cars destined for the UK market also had a Stromberg unit. Officially, no production Europa was built with Weber carburettors. Note, on the Twin Cam engine the inlet manifold is part of the head casting, so swapping from Stromberg carbs to Weber or Dellorto means changing the head.

The engine bay should be clean and tidy, with no obvious oil leaks, and neat wiring. This a Twin Cam engine bay.

Is the engine correct for the car? Some Renault-powered cars have the original engine replaced with later Crossflow variants from the Renault Fuego, or larger Federal model. The Renault-engined cars are pretty oil tight, so lots of oil may signify a problem. Check if the various drive belts are in good condition and not worn. The Twin Cam can be somewhat incontinent, so expect more oil, but the bay should not be awash with it. Cam cover leaks are not uncommon and may indicate that it's warped, but there should not be any leakage from the head gasket or the difficult-to-inspect timing chain case. Check the engine is cold, then have a peek inside the expansion bottle in the engine bay to see if the coolant is clean and to the correct level. Take off the oil filler cap and check for white 'mayonnaise,' this implies a leaking head gasket. Take out the dip stick and look at the oil: is it clean, above the minimum level marking, and are there any metallic particles in it which implies problems with the bearings.

If you take out the rear luggage box, the top of the gearbox is exposed. Is the gearbox original? The Series 1 and 2, along with the early Twin Cam had the Type 336 gearbox. The shift mechanism runs along the right-hand side (looking forwards) of the gearbox. On the Twin Cam, it was superseded by the Type 352 gearbox after the first few hundred cars. The shift mechanism runs on the left side of the gearbox. The five-speed is a Type 365, sharing the left-hand side shift mechanism with the Type 352. All the gearboxes should have a small disk bolted on the rear of the case that has the transmission type and the unit's serial number on it.

It is always worth seeing if the engine starts easily from cold, so feel (carefully) the engine to gauge its temperature before asking the owner to start it. Listen carefully for any heavy knocks from the unit, indicating main or big end bearing wear; lighter top end noise suggests out of adjustment or worn tappets. A rattle from the front of the Twin Cam or the rear of the Renault unit indicates timing chain wear. Ticking from the top end suggests the valve clearances are loose. Both units should settle down to a steady even tickover fairly quickly.

The intangibles

While carrying out an initial inspection, you should be forming some opinions about the car and if you'd want to own it. Do you feel it would suit you? Has it been well kept? Does it have the correct documentation? Can you live with it? If not, there are plenty more out there, so walk away.

The last thing to do on the initial walk-around is to step back and work out how you feel about the car. One as nice as this late Europa is well worth buying.

8 Key points
– where to look for problems

With the Europa, you must pay particular attention to a few key areas. The bodyshell will be corrosion free, but there are often problems with the paintwork and stress cracks in the gel coat. If there is obvious evidence of accident damage, or other repairs to the body, then they have not been restored properly and will need to be redone. The door hinges are prone to wear. This can be tested by looking for play: when the door is open, lift the door up against the hinge. Replacing the door hinge bearings can be tricky as the hinge pin can seize onto the bearings, which can result in damage to the bodyshell during removal.

The original Lotus chassis is made from relatively thin gauge sheet steel and can rust, especially the front and central spine. The chassis is also vulnerable to misalignment due to crash damage and is prone to cracking at the side join between the backbone and the front crossmember. Unfortunately, it's virtually impossible to see this issue with the body fitted. In general, the front and rear suspension should operate quietly, smoothly, and compliantly. Hard or sagging springs, as well as worn dampers and bushes will have a significant effect on the cars ride and handling. The bottom trunnions on the front suspension are prone to seizure if not regularly lubricated. At the rear, the fabricated steel radius arms are prone to rust, and rear wheel bearings are weak, requiring regular replacement. The car is prone to vibration if the wheels aren't balanced. If the vibration persists, the rear brake drums should also be balanced.

When looking at the bodyshell, make sure that the doors fit properly. While panel gaps tend to be wide on glass fibre cars, they should be consistent.

The Renault engine has no generic faults, but on both variants, take a close look at the cooling system to make sure it contains anti-freeze/corrosion inhibitors. Rusty water, oil, and dirty coolant are all hints that there are problems with the system.

On the Twin Cam engine, the water pump and timing chain are virtually inaccessible with the engine in place. Make sure the timing chain adjuster still has some adjustment on it, the water pump bearings are functioning and smooth, and there are no leaks from around the pump. The Twin Cam is

The Europa chassis is simple and lightweight. This is a new Lotus replacement, ready to go into a restoration project.

Carefully inspect the radiator and pipework, which can be found on the right-hand side of the front luggage compartment.

The Europa's engine bay has a removable luggage tray to its rear. This Series 1 car is original.

also prone to oil leakage. Light leakage (usually from the cam cover gasket) is acceptable and helps to protect the rear of the chassis from rust, copious amounts of oil outside of the engine is not a good sign. The oil seal, behind the alternator pulley, on the cylinder head at the rear of the engine, is a regular source of oil leaks. If the engine or gearbox mounts have deteriorated through age or oil contamination then the engine and gearbox can move excessively. This movement can cause handling of the car can be affected, with bump steer and rear wheel steering due to the use of the driveshafts as the suspension top links.

All the forward gears had synchromesh as standard, but it's often weak between first and second. Be aware that spares for Renault gearboxes are getting hard to find. Any noises, clunks, or knocks coming from this area should be treated with suspicion. The gear change mechanism from the lever to the gearbox is prone to wear.

Electrical problems and glass fibre cars go hand in hand. As the system has many more earth leads and connections than a steel car, it results in lots of potential problems.

Any fire in a glass fibre car can rapidly spread due to the inflammable nature of the bodyshell, and while repairs are entirely possible, if a fire gets hold, the car may well burn out. Electrical fires are not uncommon, so pay particular attention to the electrics. On the Twin Cam, the distributor lives below the carburettor, so any fuel leaks can be disastrous.

A tidy engine bay is important, as it shows that the owner cares about the car. This Series 2 bay has a non-standard Renault Crossflow unit installed.

9 Serious evaluation
– 60 minutes for years of enjoyment

Introduction

You've carried out the fifteen-minute evaluation, and the car is looking good. So, it's time to carry out an in-depth appraisal to see if the vehicle is what you want and to review its overall condition. The detailed inspection should be carried out methodically, do not let the seller distract you from completing all of the checks.

When you inspect the front and rear suspension, you will need to have the car jacked up. On the Series 1, there is a central jacking point under the sill and level with the rear door shut. The Series 2 and some early Twin Cam cars have front and rear jacking points on the inside edge of the sill, just behind the front and rear wheels. The later Twin Cam and Special have the jacking points on the sill behind the front wheel and in front of the rear wheel.

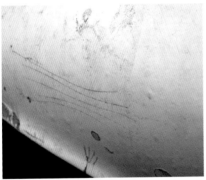

Localised damage to glass fibre bodywork can result in stress cracks that occur when the gel coat under the paint is damaged.

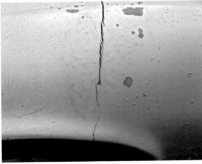

The join between the original and new panel has been filled, and has now moved, resulting in a very obvious crack.

Paintwork

Inspect the paintwork closely. It's easy to do a quick respray on a glass fibre car that looks good for a little while, but a good paint job takes time and experience, and both cost money. If the car has been resprayed recently, ask to see receipts, and make sure the bodyshop knows how to treat glass fibre repairs. See chapter 14 for a description of the main problems encountered with paintwork.

Apart from the usual paint issues (poor colour matching of repairs, fading and oxidation), there are two extra features that paintwork on glass fibre cars can exhibit. The gel coat can crack, usually around stress points such as door handles, locks, or where the bodywork has received a knock, which can result in a crack that goes through the paint and into the bodyshell itself. Poorly restored gel coat cracks will reappear rapidly, and poor repairs will be exposed by the paint sinking into them, leaving the outline of the repaired damage visible.

Blistering of the paint can occur, and, in fact, can be transitory. It can be caused by osmosis, the process of moisture permeating through the paint and gel coat and then reacting with resin and matt layers, and is often caused by leaving the car in a damp environment. The blisters will vary in size, up to 2-5mm in diameter. They may not crack the paint, and drying out the car may make the blisters disappear. However, they will reappear when the vehicle next gets damp. Micro blisters are tiny, almost pinprick-sized, and again, under the paint. Sometimes you can feel them by running your hand over the affected panel, or they may be visible by looking obliquely at the surface. They are usually caused by moisture, but also by thinners in the paint when sprayed. In either case, rectification is not difficult, but will take time and can be expensive to repair correctly.

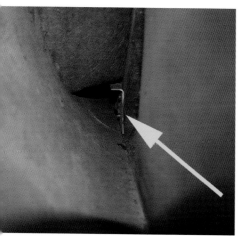

The lower outer seatbelt mounting plate can be found at the front of the rear wheelarch, and should not be rusty.

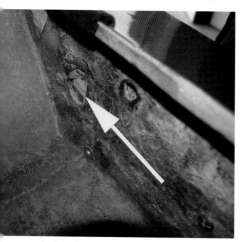

Inside the car, the lower outer seatbelt mount is positioned on the inner sill.

Bodyshell

Major repairs to the bodyshell may not be obvious, as serious damage to the shell should have been repaired by cutting out the affected panel and scarfing in a new one. This type of repair is fine, as long as the repair is done correctly. If, for example, a new front quarter has been fitted, you may feel a join under the wheelarch where the lower edges of the old and new sections meet, but you should not be able to see any evidence of the restoration. If you can see signs of a repair through the paintwork, then the job has been completed poorly and needs redoing.

Minor repairs that have been properly done will not be visible. If you can see evidence of any repairs through paint sinkage, rough areas, or obvious joins, these have not been done correctly, and will need to be reworked or redone.

While you are looking at the body, pay close attention to the seatbelt mounts. The outer ones should have a metal reinforcement plate that sits against the inner sill, and is visible if the closing panel on the front of the rear wheel well is not present: these rust and are often in poor condition. The upper outer mounts are at the top of the bulkhead. The lower inner mounts are on the transmission tunnel, and bolt through to the chassis. Give all three mounts a good inspection and physically check them, there should be no movement: If the lower centre mount is loose, there is likely to be significant corrosion on the chassis.

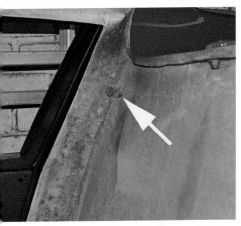

The upper outer seatbelt mounts are positioned on the rear bulkhead.

Check for stress cracks that form around hinges, door handles, on the surface of the doors, around the windscreen wiper pivots, around hatch locks, and anywhere else on the shell if it has been hit.

The doors should fit nicely with reasonable panel gaps, and fit tightly against the door seals when closed. Check for door droop, which is indicated by worn hinge bushes. Lift the open edge of the door and check for play; it should be minimal.

The front and rear compartment covers will appear to be a bit floppy when opened, this is nothing to worry about, but the front one should sit nicely on the rubber seals around the luggage compartment. This is important as the luggage compartment acts as a plenum chamber for the ventilation system.

The Europa Special should be fitted with polished metal trim that fits over the existing sills, and retained by a series of clips.

The doors are small, light, and can droop. It can be a major job to replace the hinge bushes as they tend to corrode in place.

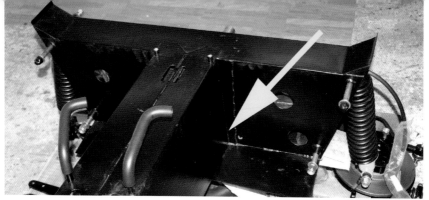

On an original chassis, cracks can develop where the crossmember is fitted to the backbone, highlighted by the arrow. On this replacement Lotus chassis, there should not be a problem as the design has been modified to strengthen the attachment point.

The Europa chassis can rust. The front of the chassis shows the front suspension pick-up points.

At the rear of the chassis, two legs splay out to support the engine and gearbox.

Chassis

The chassis is the heart of the car and can rust. To inspect it, you need to get under the vehicle and have a poke about. The rear is usually in better condition than the front, and the centre of the front crossmember is usually the worst section. Take a close look at the areas of the chassis that are visible: the bottom of the central box under the centre of the car, the ends and bottom of the crossmember at the front, and the 'Y' sections at the rear. If you find any corrosion, it will be worse in the areas you can't see. Bear in mind, it is virtually impossible to inspect the chassis without removing the body, and as a Series 1's shell is bonded, taking it off it is a major operation. On the Series 2, Twin Cam, and Special, it is still hard, but not quite as hard as on the Series 1! If the owner claims the car has had a new chassis, ask to see evidence of the purchase.

The rear of the chassis is visible in the engine bay. It's important to inspect all exposed areas for corrosion.

New rear lights and lenses for the Series 2 and onwards are available.

From a '60s Lancia, a Series 1's rear lights are rare and difficult to find.

The Series 1 and 2 had steel wheels and chrome hubcaps, which had the Lotus logo embossed in the centre.

Headlights and indicators should work and be free from corrosion. However, it's not a big or expensive job to replace them.

Lights and exterior trim

Luckily, there is little exterior trim on the Europa. Make sure that the plastic lenses on all the lights and indicators are not cracked or damaged, the chrome reflectors around the bulbs are still shiny and doing its job, and the chrome on the base plinths is in good condition. From the Series 2 and onwards, the base plinths are made from a soft zinc-based alloy, Mazak, and are almost impossible to re-chrome.

The rear lights on the Series 1 are Lancia units and very hard to find. Make sure they are in good condition. The Series 2 and Twin Cam use Lucas units that are shared with the Elan and Plus 2; the same shape unit is also used on the Jaguar E-type (Series 2 and V12), but with different light configurations. Currently, new lenses and bases are fairly easy to source. Headlights are standard 7in diameter units, which are easy to source new, as are the chromed rims around the lens. The round front indicator lenses and fittings for the Series 2 and onwards are standard Lucas items, and again, are relatively easy to source.

Do the bumpers follow the body lines closely, are they dent free, and is the chrome in good condition? Is the chrome trim around the windows and the window rubbers in good order?

Wheels and tyres

The Europa is equipped with bolt-on wheels, and, as standard, the Series 1 and 2 are fitted with 13in 4½J steel wheels with 155x13 tyres, front and rear. Steel wheels should have chrome hubcaps that fit over the nuts and have an embossed Lotus badge in the centre. The Twin Cam had the same steel wheels and tyres as the Series 2, but most were supplied with the optional Lotus-specific alloy wheels made by GKN. These were 13in diameter, but 5½J in width; the author has never seen a Twin Cam or Special with steel wheels. The alloy wheels should be fitted with 175/70x13 tyres at the front and 185/70x13 at the rear. Aftermarket wheels are not uncommon, mainly of the Minilite persuasion.

The date code for tyres is shown between the two arrows. In this case, the tyre was produced during the 47th week of 2014.

Tyres should be in good condition, with decent tread, and no cuts or tears in the sidewalls. It's worth checking the date code to see how old the tyres are. Classics often rack up only a low yearly mileage, and tyres deteriorate with age. All tyres produced since the year 2000 have a code that starts with the letters 'DOT,' which is moulded into its sidewall. This code includes a four-digit number: the first two numbers denote the week of manufacture, the last two the year. So, 2210 would indicate a tyre was produced in week 22 of 2010. If there is a three digit number, the tyre was produced before 2000, and should be replaced.

In general, it's recommended that tyres are replaced when they are 8-10 years old, so budget for a new set if this is the case.

Lotus-branded eight-spoke alloy wheels were offered as an extra on the Twin Cam and Special. They were made by GKN.

Probably the most popular aftermarket wheels are Minilites, as seen on this car.

Front suspension

The front suspension uses Triumph Spitfire/Vitesse uprights, disc brakes, top swivel joints, bottom brass trunnions, and Lotus wishbones. Inspect the wheel while it is on the ground for any damage, and look for any excessive camber, ie the wheel not sitting at 90 degrees to the road, with the top or bottom leaning in or out.

Bounce each corner to test the damper. If the dampers are in good condition, the car should rise back up to it normal level with no oscillation. With the corner jacked up, take the wheel

The general layout of the front suspension: the wishbones, Triumph-sourced upright (including the brass bottom trunnion and top ball joint), with the shock absorber sitting between the wishbones and the front roll bar.

The grey painted chassis turret should be carefully inspected for rust, as well as the disc and calliper. To the right is the radiator outlet and protective grille.

and spin it. It should spin cleanly, with no in and out, or up and down movement of the rim. If there is, then the wheel is buckled. The wheel should also spin quietly and smoothly. If not, the wheel bearings need attention. Next, take the wheel by the top and bottom (12 and 6 o'clock) and try to rock it. There should be virtually no play. If there is, the wheel bearing, top swivel, bottom trunnion, or wishbone bushes on the chassis may be worn; or the wheel nuts are loose. Check for play in the steering rack, trackrod ends, and wheel bearings by taking the wheel at 3 and 9 o'clock and rocking it. Remove the wheel and check its rear for any corrosion, dents, or damage. Also inspect all the joints on the suspension and wishbones, levering them with a screwdriver or pry bar if necessary to check for play. Next, look to see if there is any up and down movement on the bottom trunnion. Pull up on the hub while feeling if there is any movement of the upright that is relative to the brass body of the trunnion. Check the rubber bushes connecting the front anti-roll bar to the suspension. The top bushes are in the front of the wishbone spindle on the chassis, and the lower bushes are on the bottom shock absorber mount. The spring and damper unit should show no signs of oil leakage, and its top and bottom rubber mounts should be unworn.

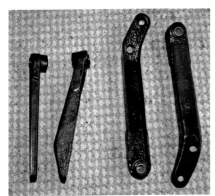

The Europa's front wishbones are made from pressed steel, with bushes in eyes in the chassis end. The left two are the upper pair and the right two the lower pair.

With the wheel off, complete the front brake inspection checks, see below. Also, inspect the wheel well, check the glass fibre bodywork for any damage, and the chassis turrets for damage or corrosion.

The front brakes are from a Triumph Spitfire, with twin-piston callipers, and solid discs. They are simple, reliable, tough, and there is not much to go wrong.

Front brakes

Check that the front disc is not scored, warped, or has any wear/ridges on its outside edge.

On early cars, the thickness of a new disc is 10mm, and 9mm when worn out. On later vehicles, the thickness of new disc is 13mm, with a thickness of 11mm when worn. If the disc has corrosion on one side, it indicates that the a piston in the calliper is sticking and needs to be rebuilt. There should be no sign of any fluid leaking from the calliper, also check the thickness of the pads. The flexible hose to the calliper should be free of any cracks or leaks.

Steering rack

You have checked for play in the rack and the trackrod ends already. The final check is to inspect the state of the rack's rubber bellows found on the front of the chassis. The rack is rigidly mounted to the front edge of the chassis, inspect the mounts for any signs of accident damage or misalignment.

The steering rack is mounted on the front of the chassis crossmember. The flexible brake hose should not show any cracking or leakage.

Rear suspension

At the rear, repeat the checks specified in the 'front suspension' section above. Check the dampers and the wheel for misalignment, warpage, or wheel

The rear suspension has a long trailing arm bolted to the hub carrier, a bottom transverse link at the rear of the hub carrier, and a coil-over damper to control vertical movement. The driveshaft acts as the top transverse link, the brake line runs along the top of the trailing arm, and the handbrake cable enters at the top of the drum backplate.

The trailing arm is fabricated from steel and can rust. This new example has the drill holes marked out for the brake pipe clips.

bearing wear. Using a jack, raise the vehicle, and repeat the tests for play in the wheel bearings. Remove the wheel and check its rear for corrosion, dents, or damage.

Check the fabricated radius arm and the brake line fixed to its top face for corrosion, and check the front mounting bush for wear. Check the chassis where the front mount is bolted for corrosion or cracking. Check the bolts connecting the radius arm to the hub for tightness.

Check the rubber bushes at each end of the lower link for wear; the inner ones often degrade due to oil contamination. Check the shock absorber's top and bottom rubber mounts for wear, and look for oil leaks. Finally, take a close look at the universal joints at each end of the driveshaft, they should be lubricated and silent in operation. Any clicking, roughness, or rust dust around the joints indicates wear. Also, inspect the wheel well, check the glass fibre bodywork for damage, examine the gearbox and engine lower casings for oil leaks or damage.

The rear suspension from the back of the car. You can see the alloy hub carrier, and the brake slave cylinder mounted on the brake's backplate, along with the lower mounts for the transverse arm and shock absorber.

Rear brakes

The cast iron rear drums will probably look tatty, but this is nothing to worry about. Take a close look at the rear of the drums, making sure the brake pipes are in good condition, and there are no leaks from the slave cylinders.

The handbrake cable goes into the back of the drum. Make sure it works by getting someone to engage handbrake while you observe the movement of the mechanism. Also, try to turn the drum when the handbrake is on.

Under the front cover

Opening the front cover exposes two compartments. At the front, the radiator nestles in the right-hand side and the spare wheel is placed in the nose. Check the radiator and its plumbing, look for leaks and general cleanliness. Take out the spare wheel and check the tyre for age, tread, and check that it matches those on the car. Note, in the case of the alloy wheels, the spare should be fitted with a 175/70 tyre.

Under the front hatch are two compartments. The front houses the spare wheel and radiator, while the rear is for luggage; it acts as a plenum chamber for the ventilation system, too.

The front compartment acts as a plenum chamber for the heating and ventilation system, and there should be a fan placed on the left-hand front of the partition between the two compartments, this pressurises the bay. Turn the fan on from inside the cabin, and check it works. There are three holes in the back bulkhead, the outer two lead to the fresh air vents in the cabin, and the centre one is the heater inlet. There should be a seal between the cover and the two compartments that should be in good condition if the heating and ventilation system is to work efficiently. In general, both front compartments should be neat and tidy. The cover's front lock should engage positively to avoid it opening while the car is in motion, and check around the hinges for stress cracks.

The engine covers on Series 1 and 2 cars had four vents.

The Twin Cam and Special had a pair of vents on the engine cover.

Under the engine cover

Firstly, ensure the engine cover is correct for the car. Renault engine covers have four vents, the Twin Cam has two. In the engine bay, check for overall tidiness and lack of oil leaks.

Behind the engine should be a removable glass fibre luggage tray. Taking this out gives great access to the top of the gearbox and rear chassis, and you should inspect both for corrosion and oil leaks. It also gives you access to the top of the exhaust system. Again, check for corrosion and any signs of blowing.

Engine

With the engine turned off, carry out a visual inspection. Check the engine mounts by rocking the engine from side to side, looking for excessive play. Then get the owner to start the engine. Listen carefully for any noise from the unit. Heavy knocks indicate severe main or big end bearing wear, while lighter top end noise suggests out of adjustment or worm tappets. A rattle from the front of the Twin Cam or the rear of the Renault unit suggests timing chain wear. Both units should settle down to a steady and even tickover reasonably quickly.

This Europa has a non-standard modern Vauxhall Twin Cam engine installed, showing how neat and clean an engine bay can be.

This Series 2 engine bay shows that there is plenty of room to inspect the gearbox and driveshafts with the luggage tray lifted out.

The original Series 1 had fixed windows made of perspex, and simple door cards.

Once the engine has warmed up, possibly after the test drive, ask the owner if you can use the compression tester on the engine. Take out all the sparkplugs, which are easily accessible on the Renault and Twin Cam engines, and spin the engine on the starter motor for a few turns with the tester in each plug hole, recording the pressure readings. All the readings should be within about five to ten per cent of each other, and above approximately 120psi. Low overall readings indicate a tired engine that will potentially need a rebore or new rings, and a top end overhaul. A low reading on one or more cylinders also suggests a problem, which again could be a ring, bore, or valve issues.

Gearbox, clutch, and driveshafts

Lift out the luggage tray, and carry out a visual inspection of the gearbox casing, looking for obvious signs of damage, cracks, repairs, and oil leaks.

Carry out the same for the bell housing. Check the clutch cable where it enters the bell housing to see if it is properly adjusted. Look at the joints in the gear change mechanism, and feel for any wear. It's worth getting someone to sit in the car to select all the gears, while you watch how the various rods and linkages operate. Feel for any play in the universal joints at each end of the driveshafts.

Interior

Take a good look at the interior, starting with the door cards, which should be free of any tears or rips.

Check that the door mechanisms work properly and operate smoothly. Make sure the electric windows work: they were never very fast, but should go up and down smoothly at a constant speed.

Check that the seat covers are in good condition, with no rips or

The electric windows on the Series 2 and onwards can be slow in operation, but rarely fail completely.

All Europas were fitted with an umbrella-handle style handbrake lever, which fitted under the dash.

The Europa's radiator is in front of the right-hand side front wheel. It should have a mesh grille to protect it.

collapsed foam, and (on the Series 2 and onwards) the seat adjuster mechanism works. Check the carpets, if they are damp, then the car is leaking. Inspect the window seals and door seals carefully. Check the wooden dashboard on Series 2 and onwards for cracks, discolouration, and lifting veneer. Make sure all the instruments and warning lights are working. The top of the dash should be free of cracks, and see if the heater fan directs air onto the windscreen. Inspect the condition of the headlining, looking for rips, or if it is drooping.

Controls

While sitting in the car, check for any slack or play in the gear change. Do the clutch, choke, and throttle cables function smoothly? Feel the brake pedal, and check the operation of the umbrella-handle style handbrake under the dash in front of the driver.

Do all the switches work properly? Check the lights, main beam, indicators, headlamp flasher, windows, fan, and horn.

Starting and running

The car should start easily. However, if it has been standing for a while, the mechanical fuel pump that is usually fitted will need to fill the carburettor. It may need a number of turns before the engine fires, but this is normal. Once started, warmed up, and the choke is pushed back in, the Renault-engined cars should settle down to a steady tickover. The Twin Cam usually won't need the choke if it is running on a Weber or Dellorto carburettor. A couple of pumps of the accelerator pedal to squirt fuel into the inlet tract is usually enough to get the engine going, but the engine may need 'juggling' on the throttle while it warms up. A Stromberg carburettor is a bit more civilised and acts like the Renault-engine cars. Once the engine has warmed up, it should rev cleanly and crisply with no hesitation or stuttering. Both engines have smooth power and torque curves, and there should be a steady progression of power up the to the red line. The Twin Cam engine should have a rev limiter fitted, but it is probably best not to test this yourself; ask the owner about it. There should be no pops and bangs in the exhaust on the overrun, an indication that the carburettor is not correctly set up. The engine should stop as soon as the ignition is turned off, with no running on. If this does not happen, it suggests there are problems with the points, or the cylinders are becoming carbonised.

Electrics

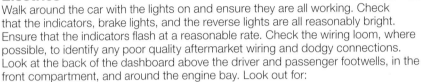

Walk around the car with the lights on and ensure they are all working. Check that the indicators, brake lights, and the reverse lights are all reasonably bright. Ensure that the indicators flash at a reasonable rate. Check the wiring loom, where possible, to identify any poor quality aftermarket wiring and dodgy connections. Look at the back of the dashboard above the driver and passenger footwells, in the front compartment, and around the engine bay. Look out for:

- Neat wiring, with no loose wires.
- Decent quality connectors. Lotus used bullet and spade connectors with soldered and crimped joins; some aftermarket connectors are not as good and should be inspected carefully.
- Any additional wires outside of the main loom clusters. What are they for? What sort of quality are they?

The use of household flex, chocolate block screw connectors, as well as wires twisted together and covered in insulation tape are a real no-no; bearing in mind the potentially disastrous results of an electrical fire.

Test drive – passenger

When taking the car for a test drive, you should split it into two halves. Firstly with you as a passenger, so you can concentrate on looking and listening out for problems, and then with you driving to assess how the car performs.

For the test drive, start off as a passenger so you can concentrate on the car, and listen and look for any problems.

During the passenger part of the test drive, check for the following:

- Look carefully at the oil pressure gauge in the cabin. Renault engines should have 60psi at normal running speeds, and between 5 and 20psi at tickover. Miles Wilkins, author of the 'Lotus Twin-Cam Engine' (see Bibliography) tells us that the Twin Cam engine only needs 45psi to run reliably at 7000rpm and normal running pressure should be between 35 and 40psi when hot. If the oil pressure is higher, quiz the owner to see if there is a high-capacity oil pump, or a modified pressure release valve fitted. Higher oil pressures will make the engine more prone to oil leaks.

- On early cars, there should be an oil pressure warning light located in the tachometer, and later vehicles had it in the dash. Start the engine and see how quickly it goes out; it should take around one second. Turn the engine off and immediately turn the ignition back on. The light should take a couple of seconds to come back on as the oil pressure drops. This test shows if the oil pressure builds up quickly and drops slowly, indicating healthy engine bearings and oil pump. If the light is not fitted, use the oil pressure gauge to carry out the test. The gauge is electrically triggered, so again, you will have to stall the engine, or turn it off then quickly turn the ignition back on.
- Listen for any knocks, rattles, or unusual noises while the car is accelerating, braking, and cornering. Try to identify where they are coming from, is it the suspension, transmission, or engine?
- Check all the instruments are working.
- Look behind the car to see if there is any blue haze, an indication that oil is being burnt. If it appears while accelerating, the rings and/or the bores are worn. If it appears on deceleration, then the valve guides are tired. Persistent white smoke indicates head gasket failure, as does the engine temperature rising with high revs and falling as they drop.
- Watch the oil pressure gauge. Fluctuating or falling oil pressure at high revs indicates worn main and big end bearings, or possibly a faulty oil pump.
- Listen for wind noise from the door seals, it should be reasonably quiet inside.
- Check the ventilation system works. Cold (ambient) air to the vents on the outside edge of the dash, and warm air to the screen and footwells.

Test drive – driver

Now swap seats and drive the car yourself, but make sure you are insured if you're on public roads. Bear in mind the Europa always had a brilliant reputation as a fast GT car with excellent handling and roadholding, even today it should perform well.

Check the following as you drive the car:
- Does the throttle work smoothly? Is it light, or notchy and stiff?
- Is the clutch reasonably light and progressive? Note, the Europa clutch is heavy compared to a modern car, but it should be smooth.
- How is the gear change? Worn linkages will make it vague and notchy.
- Does the synchromesh work on all forward gears?

Performance
- How does the car drive? Smooth and responsive, or jerky and hesitant?
- Does it accelerate quickly and evenly, or is it hesitant, jerky, and have flat spots?

Handling
- Does it keep to a line in a corner, or does it need to be continually corrected?
- Does it track in a straight line on the road, or does it fall off the camber and require frequent adjustments to maintain a straight line?
- Is the steering light, precise, and smooth, or is it heavy, notchy, and imprecise?

Brakes
- Is the brake pedal firm or spongy?
- Do the brakes have feel, or are they wooden?

- Do the brakes slow the car quickly?
- Does the car pull up in a straight line?
- Do the rear brakes lock up under heavy braking, indicating a balance problem?

Finally
- Do the speedometer, rev counter, and all the minor gauges work?
- Is the seat comfortable, or has the padding collapsed?

Once in the driving seat, enjoy the superlative handling
and road-holding of the Europa.

Evaluation criteria
Add up the total points.
80 = excellent;
60 = good;
40 = average;
20 = poor.

Excellent cars should be close to concours standard, with only a few minor faults. Good cars should be reliable runners, with a small number of faults; hopefully nothing that needs immediate attention, but the assessment should highlight any that do. Average cars will have a number of problems, both minor and major, and will need a careful assessment to inform the potential purchaser of the work required to fix them. Poor cars will potentially require a full restoration.

10 Auctions
– sold! Another way to buy your dream

Auction pros and cons

Auctions serve a useful purpose, they give owners a reliable and secure way of selling a car, and buyers the chance to purchase with minimal hassle. The price achieved is often lower than the market value, and this gives the buyers a potential bargain. Unfortunately for the buyer, cars are usually sold as seen, and there is very little comeback unless the vehicle has been wrongly described. An auction may also be used to dispose of a troublesome car, or one that needs more work than the seller is prepared to undertake.

Which auction?

It is pretty unlikely that a classic car like a Europa will appear in a normal trade-oriented auction, but not impossible, and it may be feasible to pick up a bargain if one is entered into a local modern vehicle event. However, you are much more likely to find a Europa at a specialist classic vehicle auction. The classic vehicle press usually carries adverts for these, and will often have a list of entries.

Catalogue, entry fee, and payment details

The auction catalogue usually acts as your ticket into the auction and viewing days, as well as giving limited data on all of the entries (although it may not cover those entered late). It should also provide details on how to pay (an auction will not release a car until it has been paid for and the funds verified), the buyers premium, storage costs, and any charges for credit card usage. If you are intending to go to an auction, find out in advance what the procedure is for registering, sorting out bank details or other payment methods, getting your bid paddle or number, what time the auction starts, and roughly when the cars you are interested in will be on the rostrum.

Buyer's premium

It's important to remember that the price that the car is 'hammered down to' is not the price you will have to pay. On top of the hammer price, there will be a buyer's fee, which will be a percentage of the hammer price. It is usual for there to be a local tax, such as VAT to pay on the buyer's fee as well, and you should check to see if there is any additional tax added to the hammer price. Take your time to work out what these extras add to the hammer price, and use the information to work out what your maximum bid can be.

Viewing

There are limited viewing opportunities at an auction. Some will have viewing days where you can have a good poke around, some may only allow you to see the car on the day of the auction. Either way, access to it will be limited to opening doors and lids. You may get auction staff to start the engine, but you will not be allowed to jack the car up, take off wheels, and do the sort of in-depth checks outlined in chapter 9. However, you may be able to carry out most of the initial assessment described in chapter 7. The auction staff should be able to show you any documentation that comes with the car, but one sure point is that you will not be able to take it for a test drive, and the staff will have little or no knowledge of the specific vehicle.

Bidding

At the auction itself, each car will only be on the rostrum for a short time, so make sure you know when it's due to appear. You will need to be quick and assertive with your bids, making it clear to the auctioneer that you are bidding. If the bidding goes above your limit, make it clear you are stopping bidding with a definite shake of the head. If you are successful, the auctioneer will make a note of your paddle number, and from then on, you are the owner and responsible for the vehicle. If the reserve on the car was not met, it may be possible to negotiate a sale with the seller through the auction house.

Successful bid

If you win the auction, you will hopefully have worked out beforehand how you are going to pay and get the car home. This could be driving it, using a trailer that you've bought with you, or arranging for a company to transport it for you.

If you are driving it home, it must be taxed and insured. While some insurance companies will sell limited cover insurance on-site, it's usually more cost-effective to make arrangements with your own insurance company, activating the cover over the phone if you buy the car.

eBay and other online auction sites

eBay and other online auction sites could get you a car at a bargain price, although you would be foolish to buy one without seeing and examining it.

Be aware that some cars offered for sale on eBay may be ghost cars and don't exist. Scammers will take pictures and descriptions from other websites and use them to build an eBay entry, invariably at a price well below the market rate. One way to spot these is to copy and paste the text or picture into a search engine to see if it pops up anywhere else on the web. If it does, it is likely to be a scam. If the seller is evasive or has lots of excuses as to why you can't view the car, again, this is a sure sign of a scam.

Auctioneers

The auction market can be divided into two types: national and international companies running prestigious auctions at various sites, and smaller local companies who will hold classic car auctions a few times each year in the UK and elsewhere.

The main prestigious auctions include:

Barrett-Jackson www.barrett-jackson.com; **Bonhams** www.bonhams.com; **British Car Auctions** www.bca-europe.com or www.british-carauctions.co.uk; **Christies** www.christies.com; **Coys** www.coys.co.uk; **eBay** www.eBay.com; **H&H** www.handh.co.uk; **RM Sotheby's** www.rmsothebys.com; **Shannons** www.shannons.com.au; **Silver** www.silverauctions.com.

In the UK, there are a number of well-established smaller local auction houses with regular classic car sales:

Brightwells www.brightwells.com; **Morris Leslie** www.morrisleslie.com; **Essex Classic Car Auctions** www.ecca.club; **Mathewsons Classic Car Auctions** www.mathewsons.co.uk; **South Western Vehicle Auctions** www.SWVA.co.uk; **Anglia Car Auctions** www.angliacarauctions.co.uk.

11 Paperwork
– correct documentation is essential!

The paper trail
Every car should have some sort of paper trail that will allow you to establish a car's provenance. Typical UK documentation is discussed below. Outside of the UK, local rules will apply, so make sure you familiarise yourself with them.

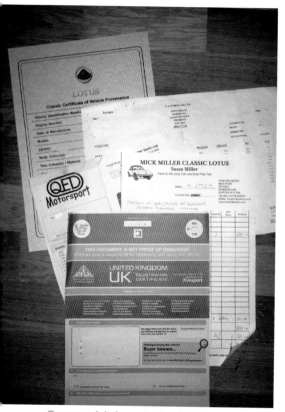

Paperwork is important as it helps to prove ownership, while contributing to the history and provenance of the car. Check it all.

Registration documents
In the UK, every vehicle used on the road must be registered using a four-page A4 document, the Vehicle Registration Certificate (V5C). It records the vehicle details, ownership details, and is used to manage the transfer of a vehicle when sold. Note, in the UK, the V5C records the registered keeper. This may not be the actual owner of the car, and therefore, is not proof of ownership. Due to new data protection legislation, it is no longer possible to acquire a list of previous owners of a car you own, or are intending to purchase, from the DVLA. This will also apply to dealerships and other specialists, from who you may wish to make contact and acquire information on previous ownership and work carried out.

Other countries have different systems, so if you need to familiarise yourself with whatever system is in operation locally.

Roadworthiness certificate
In the UK, after April 2018, all Europa cars will be over 40 years old and will not need a MoT test to be used on the road. However, if the vehicle was on the road between 2005 and 2018, its MoT history should still be available from the DVLA (www.gov.uk/check-mot-history). The site will give you its mileage when tested, along with any failures and advisories. Other countries may have local test regimes to ensure roadworthiness, and you should check the details. Some countries have

separate emissions and noise tests, so ask to see details that the vehicle will need to comply. Note, compliance with a test will only ensure the car passed on the date it was undertaken, you should satisfy yourself that it is roadworthy.

Road licence or tax

In the UK, all Europa variants are zero-rated for road tax. While you do have to have the car taxed, it doesn't cost anything. Changed legislation in the UK means that the seller of a car must surrender any existing road fund licence, and it is the responsibility of the new owner to re-tax the vehicle at the time of purchase and before the car can be driven on the road. It's therefore vital to see the V5C at the time of purchase, and to have access to the New Keeper Supplement (V5C/2), allowing the buyer to obtain road tax immediately.

Buying an imported car in the UK

If you are buying a car in the UK, and it's been imported, you'll need to follow a process to get it registered before you can use it on the road. The process does change from time to time, but at the time of publication, there are four steps you need to take:
- Tell HM Revenue and Customs (HMRC) that the vehicle has arrived in the UK.
- Pay the VAT and Duty due.
- Get vehicle approval to show that it meets safety and environmental standards.
- Register and tax the vehicle.

If the car has a NOVA (Notification of Vehicle Arrival) certificate, this indicates that the HMRC have been notified, along with the tax and duty paid. The DVLA will issue you with a used vehicle import pack (requested from www.gov.uk). You will need to provide evidence of the car's age, a MoT test (if applicable), and proof that all import taxes have been paid. Proof of age may be found on the original registration document, which will have been produced in the country the car was imported from (most USA documents contain this information). Proof of age may also be supported by a dating certificate from an authorised club, or in the Europa's case, a Club Lotus or Lotus Heritage certificate. Full details of the current process are summarised on the Federation of British Historic Vehicle Clubs website, www.FBHVC.co.uk, and the 'Driving and Transport' section of the UK Government portal, www.gov.uk.

Certificate of authenticity/Heritage certificate

Lotus can issue an official Certificate of Provenance for any of its cars produced from 1957 and onwards. The certificate includes the full VIN, model, variant, original engine and gearbox serial numbers, body and trim colours, options fitted, build date, and the original dealer or distributor. For further details and costs, contact Andy Graham at Lotus Archives: archive@lotuscars.com, telephone +44 1603 732178.

Official valuation

Some insurance companies offer agreed valuation for classic cars. Getting a valuation can be as simple as sending the insurer pictures of the vehicle, or it may involve having a professional assessment by a recognised expert. The valuation will not take into account every market fluctuation and may not match the market value of the car after it is agreed. Either way, the assessment will reflect the time and effort it would take for the owner to replace the vehicle. Therefore, the valuation may well be higher than the current market price. It also tends to cover the cost of buying a replacement from a dealer, so it'll include a premium to cover the dealer's costs. It can act as a starting point for negotiation if you are interested in buying the car, but is not a list price.

Service and restoration history

Most cars should have some sort of service history, ranging from a selection of receipts for parts and possibly notes written by the owner, to professional invoices for regular services by marque specialists. What the information should give is a picture of the previous ownership, and items such as old MoT certificates, receipts for service items (such as oil and filters) can all add to the picture.

If the car has had a full restoration, then it is not unreasonable to have supporting invoices and potentially photos of the work undertaken.

Condition

Is the car is in reasonable condition? You should have scored it using the guide in chapter 11, giving the car a condition between Excellent, Good, Average or Poor. Look at price guides published in the classic car press, these are updated fairly regularly and will give you a rough guide as to what cars are selling for in the various conditions. Most auction sites will have data on selling prices, which you should peruse to see what the cars really make. If the vehicle you are looking at is a recent show winner, this can give its value a significant boost. While originality has not been so important to the Lotus fraternity in the past, the price of original cars has been creeping up in the past few years. If originality is important to you, take a long hard look at any major modifications made to the car. Are the changes reversible? Did the seller keep the original parts so the car can be returned to standard?

It's hard to beat the classic black-with-gold-pinstripes 'John Player Special' paint scheme.

Finally, if you are buying from a dealer, they will have added a premium to cover their overheads and any warranty, and buying from an auction will include a buyers premium.

Extras and modifications

The Europa had very few extras available when new, and as such, there is little scope to add value. Probably the only desirable ones are the optional five-speed gearbox on the Twin Cam Special, and the brake servo upgrade on the Series 1a Mk1. A stainless steel exhaust system is a good addition, giving a long rot-free life. An upgraded radiator, either a re-cored original or a full replacement alloy unit is another worthwhile modification.

The presence of extras related to the car is a plus point. Items such as workshop manuals, special tools, spares, handbooks, parts lists, original magazine articles, as well as brochures and books, will not only add something to the actual value (or price) of the vehicle, but will also demonstrate an enthusiastic owner.

Significant modifications are a bit of a two-edged sword. Some will add value, some may detract value, and some will put the car into a different market sector. A popular modification to Renault-engined vehicles is the replacement of the original unit with a later one; either a 1558cc Federal unit or a Renault Crossflow. Both of these modifications are in period and don't tend to detract from the car's value. Engine and suspension tuning is another Lotus owner pastime, and the Twin Cam unit, in particular, does have considerable tuning potential. However an over-tuned engine can be a pain to use on the road or in town, and some track-oriented suspension modifications, such as stiffer dampers and higher rated springs, can ruin the car's good road manners and comfortable ride.

Spyder makes a replacement space-frame chassis made from square section tube, which is less prone to rusting than the Lotus original. They also have provision for revised rear suspension, and are generally considered to be a good alternative to the Lotus item.

The replacement of the engine with a modern unit, such as a Ford Zetec or Vauxhall Red Top, will move the car out of the classic market and into the modified market. Values of such radically modified vehicles can only be defined on a one-off basis, so are out of the scope of this guide.

Here, the original Lotus unit has been replaced by a Vauxhall engine.

Striking a deal

When it comes to agreeing on a price, your assessment of the car and its ownership history will hopefully expose any faults, and you should factor the cost of rectification into any reduction you can negotiate. However, the Europa is quite rare and does not come onto the market very often, so tying down a price can be tricky! Most owners will be enthusiasts and will have a good idea of the car's value, so negotiating can be hard!

13 Do you really want to restore?

– it'll take longer and cost more than you think

Buying a restoration project may be a way of owning a Europa at a low initial cost, but be aware of what you are getting into. The actual costs of a professional restoration will almost always exceed the value of the finished car. However, if you are mechanically able, prepared to learn how to restore glass fibre bodywork, intend to do most of the work yourself, and do not charge for your time, there is a possibility that you can complete a restoration and have a car that is worth more than your outlay. Restoring a car as a hobby is perfectly viable. As well as providing you with the satisfaction of doing all the work yourself, you know it's been restored properly. However, a full restoration will take at least twice as long and cost twice as much as your initial estimates, while consuming a great deal of time. So, if you buy a car in spring and want to run it through the summer, don't get a restoration project! A final consideration is space. As you dismantle the vehicle, you will need at least double the amount of floor space that the car requires when it's assembled, just to store the bits you have taken off. You also need to manage the area carefully, so you don't lose anything you've removed.

As this guide was being written, there were a small but steady number of barn find, and restoration projects tricking onto the market, at prices significantly below those of running cars. If you decide to buy such a vehicle, you need to ask two questions: why was the car taken off the road in the first place, and is it complete and in one piece?

A working car in excellent condition that has nothing wrong with it is rarely put into a barn or abandoned. Instead, it has likely experienced a mechanical event that

If you are looking to restore a car, you'll need plenty of space in which to work. Here, the freshly-painted Europa body is fixed on a platform out of harm's way, allowing the chassis to be stored underneath.

was not worth fixing at the time. These range from a catastrophic failure, to lots of little issues that would cause the car to not pass its next MoT test. Either way, the car will need more than just simple recommissioning to get it into a roadworthy condition. Also, consider the vehicle will have been used and was probably a typical old sports car when stored. To bring it back into good working order, it'll need a certain amount of ancillary work to the cosmetics and non-vital parts.

If the car is still in one piece and has not been stripped down, you are in a good position to assess it for completeness and condition. If you are going to take on a restoration, then it is best to assume that you will be replacing all wearing parts from the engine, gearbox, rolling chassis, and bodyshell, as well as undertaking a complete respray. Parts of the rolling chassis that degrade include suspension bushes, swivels, trunnions, springs and dampers, trackrod ends, anything that moves or rotates, and possibly the chassis. The engine may need its crank reground and a rebore, as well as a cylinder head overhaul. At a minimum, it will also require new bearings, piston rings, valve guides and seals, timing chain, water pump for the Twin Cam, and all new auxiliary belts. A carburettor overhaul will be needed, as well as overhauling the electrical system. The interior will potentially require a re-trim, along with new or repaired carpets, seat covers, door cards, dashboard, dash top, headlining, and the instruments may also need refurbishment. If the car has been left in a hot and dry environment, then it's possible that all the door and window rubbers may need replacing. Finally, the wheels will need repainting and new tyres. The elephant in the room is the bodywork, will it require a respray or can the original finish be saved? Are there any old repairs that will need to be redone?

A car that has been stripped down to its component parts has one major issue, are any parts are missing? In addition, if it's your first restoration of a Europa, you have the unenviable task of working out what all the bits in those boxes are, do they belong to the car, and how do they fit? Buying such a vehicle is a brave thing to do, and the price should reflect that!

- If you are going to take on a restoration, here are a few tips from the author:
- The main thing is to be methodical and to finish one job before starting another. When you begin to strip the car down, keep as many of the assemblies as big as possible, only breaking them down into component parts as you refurbish them. Finally, bag and tag everything you take off the car.
- Reduce the job into manageable chunks, doing one thing at a time. Group tasks into specific areas, such as those relating to the chassis and suspension, engine and transmission, and body.
- Strip down and assess the chassis. Replace or repair it.
- Refurbish the front and rear suspension, then fit it to the chassis. This gives you a rolling chassis in as new condition.
- Strip down and rebuild the engine.
- Strip down and rebuild the gearbox.
- Fit the engine and gearbox to the chassis.
- Complete bodyshell repairs and refit to the rolling chassis.
- Respray the body if needed.
- Refurbish and refit the interior trim, wiring loom, rubbers, etc.

At the end of the process, not only will you have a car that you can be proud of, but you'll have learned a lot about the Europa and how to restore cars in general!

14 Paint problems
– bad complexion, including dimples, pimples and bubbles

While the Europa's glass fibre body suggests there are no rust problems, this doesn't mean there aren't issues with the paint. Glass fibre is not as stable as steel, and this means that paintwork repairs and full resprays need a lot more preparation. Any paintwork on a Europa will take longer, and will cost more than the equivalent work on a steel-bodied car.

This is an extreme example of blistering. In this case, the integrity of the paint is compromised. Paint removal and a respray is the only option.

This is an example of micro blistering on a Series 1.

Orange peel
Appearing as an uneven paint surface and similar to the skin of an orange. It's caused by the failure of atomised paint droplets to flow into each other when they hit the surface of the panel. If the paint layer is thick enough, it is possible to rub out the effect using fine wet and dry and rubbing compound, but in severe cases, a respray is needed.

Cracking
Cracking in the paint layer is likely to be caused by paint that is applied too thickly, incorrectly mixing it before spraying, or a reaction with existing layers. If the damage is limited to the paint, it can be repaired by rubbing down and respraying the affected area. If the paint has cracked due to a damaged gel coat or glass fibre, then all the paint will have to be removed, the cracks in the gel coat or glass fibre ground out and repaired, as well as the whole area resprayed.

Crazing
Crazing is when the paint takes on the appearance of small lines and is usually caused by the same issues as cracking; repairs are the same.

Blistering and micro blistering
The appearance of blisters, small or large, and referred to in the boat industry as osmosis, is usually caused by water in the paint when the car is sprayed, or the glass fibre was damp when painted. Caused by liquid being trapped between

the glass fibre and the gel coat or paint layer, blistering will sometimes appear if the car has been kept in a damp environment or under a non-breathable car cover, disappearing once the vehicle is in a warm and dry place. The only way to prevent blistering is to keep the car in a dry environment, and making sure the bodyshell is thoroughly dried out before spraying.

Fading
When the Europa was built, Lotus initially used cellulose paint, and later moved to acrylic types. Both these paints, especially in colours at the red end of the spectrum, react to light and degrade, which causes the paint to fade. Faded bodywork may be recovered using a rubbing compound to remove the layer of damaged paint, and if successful, it should be protected with a good quality wax polish. Severe cases of fading may only be fixed with a respray.

Modern paints are a lot more stable, and fading should not be an issue if the car has been resprayed using two pack or modern water-based paint.

Peeling
Older metallic paints with a top layer of lacquer can be prone to the lacquer failing and peeling off. Poorly applied paint or inadequate preparation may also cause peeling. The only solution is to strip off the paint and respray.

Dimples/fish eyes
Dimples or fish eyes appear as imperfections in the paint layer and are caused by surface contamination, most often due to the presence of silicon-based polish. Removing the paint, cleaning the subsurface, and respraying is the only cure.

Pinstripes
When the Europa Special was produced, the pinstripes were stick-on decals and supplied to Lotus in the correct width with the corners pre-cut. The decals were light proof so were not lacquered over on the cars.

Despite its corrosion-free body, the Europa is susceptible to deterioration if it's not used regularly, as is any other car. The best advice is to take any classic on a decent run at least once a week, making sure everything that turns and burns is warmed up and exercised.

A lovely Twin Cam Special is having a great day out at a Club Lotus track day.
No worries over lack of use here!

Seized components

Any moving components have the potential to seize up through lack of use. The biggest of these is the engine, where moisture can cause the piston rings to stick to the wall of the bores. Even if the rings don't seize, corrosion on the wall of the bores can rapidly cause excessive wear, or even break one or more of the piston rings, resulting in loss of compression and excessive oil consumption. The clutch plate can corrode onto the flywheel, resulting in no clutch and potentially a damaged clutch plate when it's freed.

The Europa has clutch and throttle cables that run the length of the car, and these can fully or partially seize through lack of use and lubrication.

The pistons in the brake callipers and rear-wheel cylinders can partially or fully seize, as can the handbrake cable and mechanism.

Fuel system

The Europa's carburettors are precision instruments, and suffer if not used. If the car is left standing for a long time, all the fuel remaining in the carburettor will evaporate, leaving behind a gummy deposit. This will harden over time, and the longer it is left, the less likely that a new shot of fuel will clear it.

Fluids
Old engine oil can become acidic over time and cause damage to bearings. You can also get corrosion inside the engine if the oil is contaminated with water, which occurs when the engine is periodically started and turned off before it has warmed up. The cooling water in the engine should be mixed with antifreeze to inhibit corrosion. Brake fluid is hygroscopic and can absorb water from the atmosphere. Once water is in the system, it will corrode pistons in callipers, as well as the master, slave, and brake cylinders; corrosion can occur in steel brake lines from the inside. While silicone brake fluid is not hygroscopic, it's still worthwhile changing the fluid in the brake and clutch systems every couple of years.

Tyres
Tyres can develop flat spots causing vibration while driving along, which may be temporary or permanent. If tyres are allowed to go flat and left with the weight of the car on them, permanent damage will occur. Tyres should be replaced when they are eight to ten years old — see chapter 9 for details on how to date a tyre.

Shock absorbers or dampers
Shock absorbers will deteriorate if the car is not used. The oil reservoir seals can harden and stop working, leading to leaks.

Rubber and plastic components
Rubber and plastic components, such as windscreen wipers, gaiters, window seals, front and rear screen rubbers, suspension bushes, and cooling hoses will deteriorate with time, harden, and crack.

Electrics
Batteries do not like to be fully discharged, and will be ruined if allowed to. The many connections in the Europa's loom tend to corrode, and with its need for earthing circuits, there are many more connectors to deteriorate. The contacts inside the switches can corrode through lack of use, especially if the car is left in a hot or humid environment, or if the factory lube in them has dried out.

Exhaust system
Any exhaust system has a hard life, and on cars that see little use, condensation and combustion deposits form a corrosive mix. Luckily, the Europa's exhaust system is quite small and accessible for inspection, but it is just as susceptible to rotting as those on other cars unless a stainless steel system is fitted.

This lovely Pistachio Green Twin Cam is pictured at a Club Lotus track day.

Introduction

There are a wide range of sources for information on the Europa, ranging from books, clubs, web forums and marque specialists. In the UK, Club Lotus and the Lotus Drivers Club cater for the Europa, and both clubs hold regular local meetings and national events.

Web resources

www.lotuseuropa.org is a friendly and active forum centred around the Europa. It offers a wide range of information about the car, as well as a keen, enthusiastic, and knowledgeable membership who can answer most questions posed to them!

www.lotus-europa.com is a significant resource for the Europa owner, with lots of information on the cars, restoration, and running.

www.thelotusforums.com, as the name suggests, supports a number of forums about all Lotus cars, including a Europa thread.

Clubs

UK Clubs

Club Lotus www.clublotus.co.uk
Lotus Drivers Club www.lotusdriversclub.org.uk

USA Clubs

Golden Gate Lotus Club www.gglotus.org

Suppliers

The following suppliers all stock varying amounts of Europa (and Lotus) spares, and have either been used by the author, or have a good reputation:

Banks Europa,
Banks Service Station,
40 Church Road,
Banks,
Southport,
Lancs,
PR9 8ET.
+44 (0)1704 227059
www.banks-europa.co.uk

Mick Miller Classic Lotus,
Carlton Cross,
Main Road,
Lelsale,
Suffolk,
IP17 2NL.
+44 (0)1728 603307
www.mickmillerlotus.com

Paul Matty Sportscars,
12 Old Birmingham Road,
Bromsgrove,
Worcs,
B60 1DE.
+44 (0)1527 835656
www.paulmattysportscars.co.uk

SJ Sportscars,
Lotus House, Marsh End,
Lords Meadow Industrial Estate,
Crediton,
Devon,
EX17 1DN.
+44 (0)1363 777790
www.sjsportscars.com

The following suppliers provide spares
for the Lotus Twin Cam engines:
Burton Power,
617-631 Eastern Ave,
Ilford,
Essex
IG2 6PN.
+44 (0)20 8518 9136,
www.burtonpower.com

QED Motor Sports Ltd,
4 Soar Road,
Quorn,
Leics,
LE12 8BN.
+44 (0)1509 416317
www.qedmotorsport.co.uk

This lovely Twin Cam is ready to go on the track at a Castle Coombe Club Lotus track day.

Useful books

Lotus still produce, workshop manuals and parts books. There are also a number of books, both in and out of print, which discuss the various aspects of the Europa.

Harvey, C *Lotus: the Elite, Elan Europa*, Haynes. ISBN: 978-0902280-85-4.
A useful and informative book on the Europa, including the Elan and Elite.

Clarke, RM *Lotus Europa Gold Portfolio*, Brooklands Books. ISBN: 978-1855201-11-8.
A collection of road tests and articles on the Europa.

Robinshaw, P., & Francis, D *The Lotus Europa Derivatives and Contemporaries 1966-1975*, RB Publications. ISBN: 978-0952808-61-9.
A celebration of the Europa and its racing cousins, with lots of important details about the cars, as well as reprints of contemporary brochures and articles.

Herzog, B *Europa Euphoria*. ISBN: 978-0615641-19-5.
A self-published, nice, amusing little book, chronicling the restoration of a 1973 Twin Cam Special.

Whittle, K *Lotus 46 – The Europa S1*.
A self-published book with some history of the Europa, reprints of factory and road tests, and owners' stories.

Newton, R, & Psulkowski, R *Lotus The Elan, Cortina and Europa*, Tab Books. ISBN 978-0830621-06-4.
Good coverage of the Europa alongside the Elan and Lotus Cortina.

Wilkins, M *Lotus Twin-Cam Engine*, Brooklands Books. ISBN: 978-1855209-68-8.
A recent reprint of the definitive guide to the design, development, rebuilding, and maintaining of the Lotus Twin Cam engine.

Lotus owners are a friendly bunch, and happy to talk to people about their cars. Here, a Twin Cam has an appreciative audience at a Club Lotus event.

17 Vital statistics
– essential data at your fingertips

Dimensions

	Europa Series 1	Europa Series 2	Europa Twin Cam
Length	399.4cm/157.25in	399.4cm/157.25in	400cm/157.5in
Height	107.9cm/42.5in	107.9cm/42.5in	107.9cm/42.5in
Width	163.8cm/64.5in	163.8cm/64.5in	163.8cm/64.5in
Wheelbase	231.1cm/91in	231.1cm/91in	233.7cm/92in
Weight	612kg/1350lb	710kg/1566lb	712kg/1570lb
Fuel capacity	32l/7gal/8.4 US gal	32l/7gal/8.4 US gal	56l/12.5gal/15 US gal
Wheels and tyres	155x13	155x13	175x13 Front 185x13 Rear

Production numbers
A lot of the original Lotus production records were lost when the archive was flooded, but, by comparing various sources and the looking at the Lotus chassis numbering system, the following values are a reasonable approximation of the actual numbers of cars produced:

Series 1: 296
Series 2: 1788
Twin Cam: 1567

Series 1 Mk2 (also referred to as S1A/B): 346
Series 2 Federal: 2506
Twin Cam Special: 3383

Giving a grand total of approximately 9886 Europas produced in total between 1967 and 1975.

Lotus Type numbers
The Series 1 Europa was assigned the Lotus model designation Type 46, Series 2 cars Type 54, the Federal specification Series 2 with the 1565cc engine were Type 65, while the Twin Cam and Special models were Type 74.

Chassis/VIN
Until the end of 1969, the Europa's VIN was in the following format: 46/0001. '46' is the Lotus Type number, and '0001' is the unit number. According to the official Lotus Workshop manual, Series 1 cars started at 46/0001 running to 46/0299, Series 1 Mk1 cars ran from 46/0300 to 46/0644, Series 2 cars started at 54/0645, Series 2 Federal started at 54/1066, and 1565cc Federal Cars ran through from 65/0001 through to 65/2952.

From January 1970, Lotus changed its numbering system to conform to international standards. The new system was in the following format: 7001.991234A. '7001' represents the year (1970) and Month (01-January), '9' is the production batch, '234' is the unit number, and 'A' is the model. In the Europa's case, this should be P, Q, or R. 'P' indicates a UK specification Europa, 'Q' a Standard Export model, and 'R' a Federal Export model.

Engine details

	Renault	Renault – Federal	Twin Cam (Special)
Type	All alloy, four-cylinder, in-line	All alloy, four-cylinder in-line	Cast iron block, alloy cylinder head
Bore and stroke	76mm x 81mm	77mm x 84mm	82.55mm x 72.75mm
Capacity	1470cc	1565cc	1558cc
Carburettor	Solex 35 DIDSA 26mm Twin Choke	Solex 26-32 Emissions	Twin Dellorto 40 DHLA
Compression ratio	10.25:1	10.25:1	9.5:1 (10.3:1)
Power	78bhp@6000rpm	80bhp@6000rpm	105bhp@6000rpm (126bhp@6500rpm)
Torque	76ft/lb@4000rpm	79ft/lb@4000rpm	103ft/lb@4500rpm (113ft/lb@5500rpm)
Valve gear	Pushrod operated, two valves per cylinder	Pushrod operated, two valves per cylinder	Double overhead cams operating two valves per cylinder (big-valve head)

A classic Lotus Europa Twin Cam in classic Lotus colour.

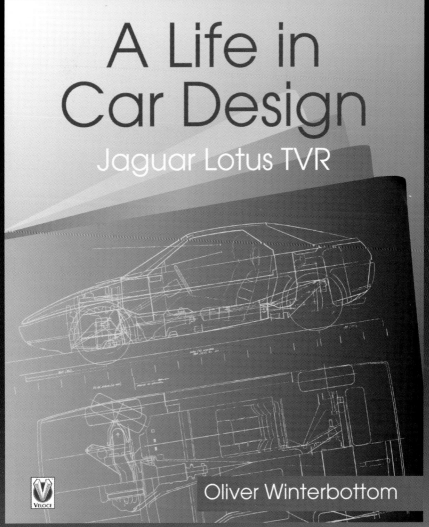

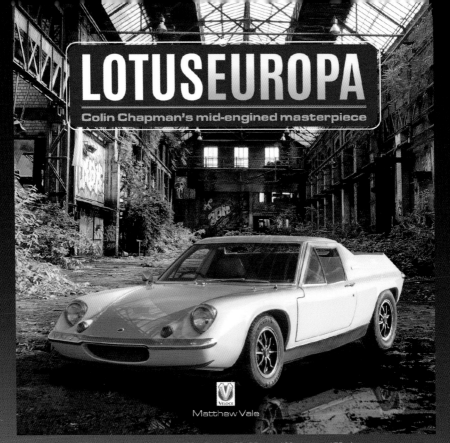

The Essential Buyer's Guide™ series ...

... don't buy a vehicle until you've read one of these!

Index